First World War
and Army of Occupation
War Diary
France, Belgium and Germany

59 DIVISION
Divisional Troops
Machine Gun Corps
200 Battalion
1 August 1918 - 31 October 1918

WO95/3017/12

The Naval & Military Press Ltd
www.nmarchive.com
Published in association with The National Archives

Published by

The Naval & Military Press Ltd

Unit 10 Ridgewood Industrial Park,

Uckfield, East Sussex,

TN22 5QE England

Tel: +44 (0) 1825 749494

www.naval-military-press.com

www.nmarchive.com

This diary has been reprinted in facsimile from the original. Any imperfections are inevitably reproduced and the quality may fall short of modern type and cartographic standards.

© **Crown Copyright**
Images reproduced by permission of The National Archives, London, England, 2015.

Contents

Document type	Place/Title	Date From	Date To
Heading	WO95/3017/12		
Heading	59 Div Troops 200 Bn Machine Gun Corps 1918 Aug-Oct		
War Diary	Belton Park Grantham	01/08/1918	26/09/1918
War Diary	South Ampton	27/09/1918	27/09/1918
War Diary	Le Havre	28/09/1918	30/09/1918
War Diary	Berguette	01/10/1918	01/10/1918
War Diary	Guarbecque	02/10/1918	02/10/1918
War Diary	Le Gorgue	03/10/1918	04/10/1918
War Diary	Rouge-De-Bout	05/10/1918	05/10/1918
War Diary	Fleurbaix	06/10/1918	17/10/1918
War Diary	Fme De La Hallerie	18/10/1918	18/10/1918
War Diary	La Madelaine	19/10/1918	19/10/1918
War Diary	H E M	20/10/1918	23/10/1918
War Diary	Orchies.	24/10/1918	31/10/1918
Miscellaneous	Appendix I.	01/08/1918	01/08/1918
Miscellaneous	Appendix. II. Officers of No.280 M.G. Company.	06/09/1918	06/09/1918
Miscellaneous	Appendix. III. Officers of A. Coy. 280 M.G. Battalion	17/10/1918	17/10/1918
Operation(al) Order(s)	Operation Orders. No.1. App IV		
Operation(al) Order(s)	No. 200 M.G. Battalion. Operation Order No. 2.		
Operation(al) Order(s)	No. 200 M.G. Battalion. Operation Order No. 5.		
Operation(al) Order(s)	No. 200 M.G. Battalion. Operation Order No. 3.		

w095
3017/12

59 DIV TROOPS

200 BN ~~MOTOR~~ MACHINE GUN CORPS

1918 AUG - OCT

WAR DIARY
or
INTELLIGENCE SUMMARY.
(Erase heading not required.)

Army Form C. 2118.

Instructions regarding War Diaries and Intelligence Summaries are contained in F. S. Regs., Part II. and the Staff Manual respectively. Title pages will be prepared in manuscript.

59

1/200 Bn M.G.C.

Place	Date	Hour	Summary of Events and Information	Remarks and references to Appendices
BELTON PARK GRANTHAM.	1.8.18	—	On August 1st 1918, the 200th M.G. Battalion was formed in the E. Linden Belton Park Grantham and was composed of 49 Officers 862 Other Ranks A, B, C & D — and Transport made up in four companies A, B, C & D.	* App. I Names of Officers.
BELTON PARK GRANTHAM	6.9.18	—	According to W.O. order, on the 6th Sept. 1918, A Company ceased to be known as 280. M.G. Coy *. Then company was again split up for service in North Russia. to which front it will proceed.	* App. II Names of Off. 4) 280 Coy.
BELTON PARK GRANTHAM	17.9.18	—	In accordance with W.O. Instructions a new company was formed on this date to duty became A. Coy. * replacing 280 M.G. Coy.	* Ap. III Names of Officers A Coy.
BELTON PARK GRANTHAM	18.9.18	—	No 280 Coy. Left Belton Park Camp and entrained at GRANTHAM STATION on route for LEITH at 12.37. A.M. 18.9.18	
BELTON PARK GRANTHAM	26.9.18	—	The Battalion proceeded to Southampton en route for France embarkment commencing at 11.30 P.M. and being completed at 6.10 A.M. 27.9.18	
SOUTHAMPTON	27.9.18	—	The personnel of the Battalion embarked on the S.S. KING EDWARD for HAVRE. The transport, 3 Warrant Officers and 40 O.R.s proceeded to HAVRE on the S.S. NIRVANA. The S.S. King E. berthed at HAVRE at 4.45 A.M. 28.9.18. after an extremely rough crossing.	
LE HAVRE	28.9.18	—	The Battalion marched from the quayside to No 1 A Rest Camp at SAINT ADDRESSE and were detailed in tents. The S.S. NIRVANA having encountered the heavy seas in St. but it until late the noon night.	

WAR DIARY
or
INTELLIGENCE SUMMARY.
(Erase heading not required)

Army Form C. 2118.

Instructions regarding War Diaries and Intelligence Summaries are contained in F.S. Regs., Part II. and the Staff Manual respectively. Title pages will be prepared in manuscript.

Place	Date	Hour	Summary of Events and Information	Remarks and references to Appendices
LE HAVRE	30.9.18	—	The Battalion entrained in two parties as shown to proceed to BERGUETTE (N⁰ AIRE.) N⁰ 1 PARTY. A & C Coys, & H-Q. - 8.30. A.M. " 2 " B & D " - 12.30 P.M.	Appendix IV O.R. N⁰ 1.
BERGUETTE	1.10.18	—	The Battalion detrained at BERGUETTE and marched into billets about three miles distant at LE PERRIÈRE, Batt. H-Q. at GUARBECQUE.	
GUARBECQUE	2.10.18	—	Orders were received from XI⁰ Corps to move to LA GORGUE (about 3½ miles E. of MERVILLE) and the personnel of the battalion proceeded there by lorry, but transport went by road. The night of the 2/3. Oct. the battalion bivouacked at LA GORGUE in the vicinity of the H-Q. of N⁰ 61. M.G. BATTN. with which it was temporarily attached. At that time the XI⁰ Corps were on the line running from its S. ARMENTIÈRES to FROMELLES, the 61ˢᵗ DIVISION being on the LEFT (or NORTH) and its 59ᵗʰ DIVISION on its RIGHT. The left of the 61ˢᵗ DIVISION M.G. BATT. and the 61ˢᵗ M.G. BATT. was covered by the right 9ᵗʰ Infantry 9ᵗʰ 61ˢᵗ DIVISION by the 59ᵗʰ DIV. and the relief of the 59ᵗʰ DIV. by the 47ᵗʰ DIV. From the 2ⁿᵈ Oct. the 59ᵗʰ DIV. commenced an attack to decrease its 59ᵗʰ DIV. Oct. then took its branches, the 2005 M.G. Battn. becoming attached to it in the direction of LILLE which was receiving effective machine gun assistance as they fell back, the Germans carried out being closely followed by our troops. An Army of destruction of everything in the nature of retreat, but intercepts and a system alike all kinds being in the grounds.	
LA GORGUE.	3.10.18	—	In the early morning 150 men from N⁰ 61. Battn. to assist in the Corps line were sent their reinforcements by A & C. Companies.	

WAR DIARY
or
INTELLIGENCE SUMMARY.
(Erase heading not required.)

Army Form C. 2118.

Instructions regarding War Diaries and Intelligence Summaries are contained in F.S. Regs., Part II. and the Staff Manual respectively. Title pages will be prepared in manuscript.

Place	Date	Hour	Summary of Events and Information	Remarks and references to Appendices
LE GORGUE	3.10.18 (cont)		Later in the day B & D Companies moved up to form ?? positions in the line. B. Coy was attached to No 176 Bde — D Coy to No 177 Bde which its O.C. D. Coy was moving forward with this from action officers a much revised Coy by the actual 2/Lt morning, composed — Killing Major LAIN & assuming LT BEAVIS, 2/Lt BLACK & Lt ALMON. LT BEAVIS, who was only slightly wounded, returned to duty the next day.	App V OP. No 2
LE GORGUE	4.10.18		Nothing to report during morning, - at 3-30 PM advanced Battalion H-Q moved forward to ROUGE DE BOUT and in the course of the evening C. Company moved up with business to Batt H-Q. Enemy activity on the Division's front was practically nil - with the exception of slight artillery action in the vicinity of FLEURBAIX - S.W. of ARMENTIERES.	
ROUGE-DE-BOUT	5.10.18		Slight advance was made by our troops during the morning and patrols found little opposition for about 200 yds — machine gun fire was encountered N & S. 1000 yds E. of WEZ MACQUART and the line was established running about 500 yds W of that village. A. Coy came up at 1.15 P.M. and was relieved by C. Coy at ROUGE-DE-BOUT. Batt H-Q moved from ROUGE-DE-BOUT to GERMAN huts S.W. of FLEURBAIX.	
FLEURBAIX	6.10.18		A further slight advance was made during the day - an infantry patrol which ??? A & C) Coys moved up ???? which was filled in LARGE FARM and DISTILLERY. The enemy seems inclined to evacuate FLEURBAIX awaiting further action before launching any large ???? patrol. The action though line of one or two pieces - machine guns BOIS-GRENIER village which received a good deal of attention with BLUE-CROSS gas shell.	

Army Form C. 2118.

WAR DIARY
or
INTELLIGENCE SUMMARY.
(Erase heading not required.)

Instructions regarding War Diaries and Intelligence Summaries are contained in F.S. Regs., Part II. and the Staff Manual respectively. Title pages will be prepared in manuscript.

Place	Date	Hour	Summary of Events and Information	Remarks and references to Appendices
FLEURBAIX	7.10.18		Pat. were again sent out during the day - one patrol was fired upon by M.G's from INDEED TRENCH and another shelled at E. of WEZ MACQ. App. VI U.A.R.T. During its afternoon reconnoitre hostile artillery was very active. O.P. No.3. Relief of the three divisions of front was carried out by the V on its day, as shown on O.P. No. 3.	
FLEURBAIX	8.10.18		Nothing of note occurred during the day - hostile artillery was active and a good deal of retaliation opened up with its fire from the batteries E. of WEZ MACQUART. Examination of prisoner of 6th I.R. 56. DIVISION shows that division is holding LILLE and its suburb - ST. ANDRÉ - LA MADELAINE and LAMBERSART. This evacuation was noticed by prisoner on 3.10.18.	
FLEURBAIX	9.10.18		During the night 8/9 the enemy attempted to raid our left front division but his effort was unsuccessful. It was frustrated by the N. LANC. front W. of SANTES who captured a prisoner. During its evening of the 8th a successful raid was made on the enemy's saps of WEZ - MACQUART and captured a prisoner.	
FLEURBAIX	10.10.18		Situation unchanged although its day - patrols were very active - an attempt was made during the day to enter the front of its enemy in front of its outpost line but he was found still held by the enemy T.M's.	
FLEURBAIX	11.10.18		Patrols out during the day - sent out to ascertain here established his outpost line in ? WEZ MACQUART and establish touch with him. It was ascertained from information in the N. of the village that the enemy still holds the village E. of its village itself in battalion ? in	

WAR DIARY
or
INTELLIGENCE SUMMARY
(Erase heading not required.)

Army Form C. 2118.

Place	Date	Hour	Summary of Events and Information	Remarks and references to Appendices
FLEURBAIX	11.10.18	(Cont)	Lettern may be. Prisoners taken state that evacuation of LILLE and intermediate villages continued and that others are being carried out quietly on parties. An announcement made by PRESIDENT WILSON is a fear for peace on the part of GERMANY rejected the request for an armistice on the grounds of such a thing being purely a military action which should be decided by its military advisors of the ENTENTE powers. The also mentioned his conditions to which GERMANY must adhere if he is to recommend her peace overtures to statesmen concerned to endorse his reply even with the highest approval.	
FLEURBAIX	12.10.18		On its whole front the enemy seems to have withdrawn and is being followed up by our infantry patrols. They did not everywhere immediately evacuate their places and were generally shelling heavily our advancing troops which are finding it hard to maintain touch with him. Considerable movement and activity has been reported on the N.W. outside Gen. PLUMER, which made by enemy on the North of a good deal on the enemy South LILLE in the head of a worthy formed.	
FLEURBAIX	13.10.18		Minor operations towards ERQUINGHEM - WEZ MACQUART resulted in the capture of 22 prisoners. A hostile attack developed on one the position gained and our troops were forced to withdraw. Enemy patrols of prisoners taken back of the Lille area state that LILLE will shortly be in enemy hands - statement in connection with this article is doubted for an attempt are on history.	

Army Form C. 2118.

WAR DIARY
or
INTELLIGENCE SUMMARY.
(Erase heading not required.)

Instructions regarding War Diaries and Intelligence Summaries are contained in F. S. Regs. Part II. and the Staff Manual respectively. Title pages will be prepared in manuscript.

Place	Date	Hour	Summary of Events and Information	Remarks and references to Appendices
FLEURBAIX	13.10.18 (cont)		During the day an intc. company relief took place. 'B' Coy. relieving 'A' Coy. and 'D' Coy. relieving 'C' Coy. *	* App. VII O.P. Nos-
FLEURBAIX	14.10.18		No change on divisional front - more intermittent wire cutting activity on either side. Enemy attempting through the day however an increase on the part of its artillery which replied with decreasing vigour and intensity an unusual occurrence. There seems some indication that the enemy is preparing to withdraw to a line E. of LILLE. This was indicated to us by a hostile telegraph order to locate & locate positions on the CORPS LINE of defences. Reconnaissance by the C.O. and Quarter Master of future positions for the Bn. continued throughout the day. Telephone rules & telephone centres tried & time.	
FLEURBAIX	15.10.18		Enemy evacuation of Army front expected to-day - strong evidence that its withdrawal has taken place from HAUBOURDIN northwards. Low flying aeroplanes sent over enemy lines and no M.G. fire was directed on them, pointing to the fact that with the exception of the rear guards all the troops have been withdrawn. Orders from 69th Division were received by the Division & Bn. to be ready to move forward and send out the company on an hour notice after 6.30. AM. 16.10.18. The 2nd Army report that its advancing in its vicinity of HENIN, WERVICQ and COMINES. 1st Army is still advancing in the vicinity of DOUAI. German reception of PRESIDENT WILSON's reply to PEACE NOTE reported to have been very disspirited. TURKEY would like to detach herself from GERMANY with the effect that she will be able to stand on neutrals here with ENTENTE powers	

WAR DIARY
or
INTELLIGENCE SUMMARY.
(Erase heading not required.)

Army Form C. 2118.

Instructions regarding War Diaries and Intelligence Summaries are contained in F. S. Regs., Part II. and the Staff Manual respectively. Title pages will be prepared in manuscript.

Place	Date	Hour	Summary of Events and Information	Remarks and references to Appendices
FLEURBAIX	16.10.18		Enemy withdrew and commenced our troops moving forward. During its retirement it seems enemy to the vicinity of CHAPELLE ARMENTIERES, which was destroyed and covered - A Coy moving. The forward companies were in contact with reported Enemy patrols by the hotels up the enemy advanced, in apparently weakening. It was decided not to push up the troops from their present positions. The C.O. accompanied H.Q. selecting a place at Fme DE LA HALLERIE.	
FLEURBAIX	17.10.18		During the morning Batta H.Q and C Coy (in reserve) moved up to FME DE LA HALLERIE, arriving about 11.30 A.M. The advance continued on its Army front and Btk forces continued patrols reported. Our troops entered the town of LILLE and reported its enemy had shelled. It had practically no civilians and nothing more could be obtained upon its enemy - old civilians say the greatest enthusiasm was shown upon its entry. Reports from all civilians informed that the GERMANS completed a retirement to ensure its hostile towards the evening A. C. Coys encountered enemy patrols towards the line KLEMEHIN E of TOURNAI. During the evening Bn H.Q remaining at FME DE LA HALLERIE.	
FME DE LA HALLERIE	18.10.18		Batta H.Q and A.C Coys moved forward to ST ANDRE - N of LILLE. The advance continued and enemy fresh from its front, occupying a strong position built patrols found the enemy. They destroyed inland, and were attacked. Its advance was to swing up the position.	

WAR DIARY
or
INTELLIGENCE SUMMARY.
(Erase heading not required)

Army Form C. 2118.

Place	Date	Hour	Summary of Events and Information	Remarks and references to Appendices
(Cont)	18.10.18		the enemy did not put up much resistance. ROUBAIX and TOURCOING were liberated by the 1st infantry and were left at 6.10 P.M. Batt H-Q headed to move forward from ST. ANDRE to LA MADELAINE which move was carried out by 11.30 P.M. A & C Coys also came up and settled in the vicinity of Batt H-Q. Report from mule circles are a part from the enemy states that the enemy are retreating rapidly on a front from SAILLY LES LANNOY and WILLEMS and that its covering rear guard are moving back customarily. So far bridges over RIVER SCHELDT remain intact - East continual by air & plane.	
LA MADELAINE	19.10.18		The advance continued to-day and was reported as being in the line reported either expectations. An the evening to the city to be carried out on the 19th had to be called off owing to the notice from and movement. Dinants on left and right up and preparing. Cavalry patrol's reported enemy cleared from FOREST de LILLE, in which place they were making some resistance. About mid-day Batt H-Q and the two advance paining coys received by 8.0. P.M. Report forward to HEM and the move was completed by 8.0. P.M. Report on to the enemy situation received which states certain care is drawn from Hem. Evidence points to the fact that enemy is being drawn back to line on the East bank of the SCHELDT RIV - but owing to the fact that a some number bridges have going to Hem up employed. frm the N of it in particular ER.- they noting it is drawn to a line between ATH will be drawn to a line between ATH	

WAR DIARY
INTELLIGENCE SUMMARY

Army Form C. 2118.

Place	Date	Hour	Summary of Events and Information	Remarks and references to Appendices
(continued)	19.10.18		East of TOURNAI.	
H.E.M.	20.10.18		Enemy withdrew al along the line NECHIN - TEMPLEUVE during the night of the 19th. The enemy was reported to be holding W. bank of RIVER SCHELDT. A Coy and C Coy relieved B Coy and D Coy respectively and the relief was complete by 10.0 A.M. 20th The whole of the relief was carried out of view of enemy and observatory - and the relieving companies went through them taking up their positions with the forward infantry companies. Enemy shelling increased during the day and TEMPLEUVE - RUMEZ ROAD shelled at intervals - also the TEMPLEUVE - RUMEZ ROAD but there was no shelling of back areas. Reports from civilians show that a large amount of transport at leaving TOURNAI and ANCOING is believed to be going to BRUSSELS. Every report states enemy still holding western bank of RIVER SCHELDT. Further reports show that the civilian population of TOURNAI has been ordered to evacuate the town by 12.00 NOON to-day.	
H.E.M.	21.10.18		The brigade reconnaissance was made to find forms and ascertain the nihe during the afternoon, and intelligence reports showed that the N. of TOURNAI. Palais eveneum again seminal the	

WAR DIARY
INTELLIGENCE SUMMARY.
(Erase heading not required.)

Army Form C. 2118.

Place	Date	Hour	Summary of Events and Information	Remarks and references to Appendices
(Cont)	2/10/18		morning but little progress was made by the main body. Morning report stated R.E.'s making bridges across RIVER SCHELDT at various points. From our forward companies reports were received that enemy T.M.'s were active indicating that forward line of advance was close up to enemy rear guard. During the afternoon 170 Bde, 57 Division relieved 178 Bde. of the 59th Division – C Coy remain with its own Brigade.	
HEM.	22/10/18		Reports show that enemy is still holding W. bank of the RIVER SCHELDT. Attempts made to cross the river were unsuccessful except at a few points where smell parties were temporarily established. The enemy appears to be making a strong stand on this and to get this we got his Transport took. Strong patrols crossed the RIVER SCHELDT by greater linkage from the L. Bou at PONT A CHIN and proceeded about 300 yds east of the river – they met with every strong opposition from PARADIS and the RAILWAY EMBANKMENT and were driven back. On the night of 22ND/23RD strong patrols were sent out from the Right Bn and they cleared the WOOD south of PONT A CHIN and the Point of the bayonet and established posts in the CONVENT and were fired on by M.G.'s	
HEM.	23/10/18		The enemy is holding the W bank of the RIVER SCHELDT still and have a series of posts on the E of the railway. His M.G. are very active and a lot of snipering is being done by him. Sniper fires have been noted on and beyond the railway. The C.O. reconnoitred for new Bn. H.Q. and selected a point at ORCHIES. The H.Q.	

WAR DIARY
or
INTELLIGENCE SUMMARY.
(Erase heading not required.)

Army Form C. 2118.

Place	Date	Hour	Summary of Events and Information	Remarks and references to Appendices
HEM.	23/10/18		Moved up during the morning with C Coy (in reserve) to ORCHIES arriving about 11.30 a.m. Bn. H.Q. was opened at 12 noon. — Reports received show that civilians are still in TOURNAI. Our advance still delayed owing to vulnerability of bridges. C Coy H.Q. at BUVRIÈRE FARM. Evening report — Sitn unchanged and fairly quiet. E of SCHELDT we have established posts. Enemy artillery active shelling W. Bank of RIVER SCHELDT. Enemy Aircraft active with our flying on lines. Our A.A. fire + 18 pars fired on movement E. of SCHELDT at OBIGIES. Slight hostile shelling at RAMEGNIES. CHIN area also T.M's. Shelling of rural scattershot by Minnies and Shrapnel T.M's & Pdrs.	
ORCHIES.	24.10.18		Enemy still holding same line East SCHELDT. Hostile artillery somewhat active — Slight 'GAS' shelling — M.G. fire slight — Snipers busy. Enemy M.G. captured by 2/Lt PROCTER of 11th Scot. L.I. at about 900x N.E. of RAMEGNIES-CHIN. — Some trenches and wire defences are being constructed by enemy at suitable points on E. of SCHELDT. Enemy line appears to run through HARRON and Northwards to OBIGIES. and small gaps running Nwd by roads thence S.E. of FARINETTE — New trenches are seen at HAVRON and rifle pits at HARRON. Front comparatively quiet today. Slight shelling of our forward area.	
"	25.10.18		Situation today is unchanged on 59th DIVISION FRONT. Hostile ARTY + MG quieter than usual — Casualties were made by 4 O.R. and a light M.G. at a Point about 1500x N of POINT A CHIN.	
	26.10.18			

WAR DIARY
or
INTELLIGENCE SUMMARY.
(Erase heading not required.)

Army Form C. 2118.

12

Place	Date	Hour	Summary of Events and Information	Remarks and references to Appendices
ORCHIES	27/10/18		Front is still unchanged but hostile Artillery and machine guns are becoming more active. It would seem that it is the intention of the enemy to hold this line until eventualities on either flank cause him to retire. Fire from LA TOLIE & heavy machine gun fire and from the WINDMILL 500's S of HAVRON. Ay 2353 the XI Corps mounted troops came under the orders of this DIVISION. In the night of the 27/28th an inter Bgd relief took place – (B & D Coys relieving A & C Coys respectively) taking over the same gun positions & lines. During relief heavy M.G. fire from HAVRON. On line and suburbs were fairly active.	
"	28.10.18		Relief complete by 04.00 hrs on 28th inst. Hostile M.G. & Arty fairly active – BAILLEUL and also N of L shelled by M.m.s & 4.2s (some with GAS.) TEMPLEUVE was also shelled with gas shells – Concentration of enemy troops and transport was reported at CABT LIETARD – on which and heavy Artillery crashed this point. The Infantry sent out patrols to ascertain results – they saw one or two of enemy who immediately bolted.	
"	29/10/18		Situation unchanged on DIV. FRONT. Hostile Arty more active. Divisions on left and right are meeting with the same resistance but have established posts on E bank of SCHELDT. Enemy appear to be moving transport back as fast as possible and it would appear that he is not preparing to retire to a line further back, even tho' he is not apparently going until he is forced.	
"	30.10.18		Situation unchanged throughout the day. No further enemy columns being made – Infantry Patrols went out but not with decisive results. Enemy Aircraft active, especially low flying planes.	

WAR DIARY
or
INTELLIGENCE SUMMARY.

Army Form C. 2118.

Place	Date	Hour	Summary of Events and Information	Remarks and references to Appendices
ORCHIES.	30.10.18 (contd.)		The enemy using tracer bullets from M.G's when firing at any movement and it would appear that he is doing this to direct the Artillery on that point as they open fire on the point where the bullets appear to strike almost immediately. Harassing fire was carried out by our M.G. during the night of the 30th/31st.	
"	31.10.18	—	No further advance made — Front comparatively quiet — Some gas shelling in forward areas — GAS is being used more frequently during the last day or so — evidently the enemy in getting rid of dumps (preparatory to retiring.) — DIVISIONAL H.Q. (59th) move back from ESTAFFLERS to SAILLY-LEZ-LANNOY today and re-opened at 12.23 hrs. From information received from 11th Corps a satisfactory armistice has been arranged with TURKEY to come into force from 12 noon today	

APPENDIX I.

1.8.18.   Sheet I

Names, ranks & appointments of Officers of 200. M.G. Battn.

NAME & RANK.	APPOINTMENT	REMARKS
Lt-Col. A.P. Evans. D.S.O.	Officer Commanding.	
Major. G.E. Wilkinson. M.C.	2/nd. in Command	
" H.H. Dawes.	O.C. A. Company.	
" E.E. Spencer.	" B "	
Capt W. Wilson.	" C "	Since promoted Major.
" J.G. Laing.	" D "	Since promoted Major.
" G.I. Wicks. MC	Adjutant Battn.	
" T.D. Hallman.	2/I.C. C. Company	
" F.C. Russon-Bayliss. MC	" " A "	
Lt. S.H. Gelvard. MC	" " B "	Since promoted Capt.
" J.R.C. Rankine.	" " D "	Since promoted Capt.
" O.H. Dixon.	Headqrts Transp. Officer	
" F. Michelmore.	Asst Adjt & Int. Off.	
" I. Clarke. R.A.M.C.	Medical Off.	
" J.E. Walker.	Battn. Quartermaster	
" E.A. Sturt.	Sect Off. A Coy	
" R.S. Willmer.	" " " "	
" R.B. May.	" " " "	
" R. Affleck.	" " " "	
" L.V.H. Saquin.	" " B "	
" J.H. Wilson.	" " " "	
" M.J. Treynitha.	" " " "	
2/Lt N. Hardy.	" " " "	
Lt. H. Glyn-Jones.	" " C "	
" J.P. Klosberg.	" " " "	
" J.R. Gregory.	" " " "	
2/Lt A.F. Thomas.	" " " "	
Lt. E.S.P. Almon.	" " D "	
" S.J.S. Beavis.	" " D "	
2/Lt W.H. Black.	" " " "	
" J.B.W. Travis.	" " " "	
" E.C. Bradfield	Sub. Sect Officer. A.	
" J.B. Mills.	" " " A.	
" T.B. Graham	" " " B.	

APPENDIX I (Cont)   Sheet II.

1.8.18.

NAME & RANK.	APPOINTMENT	RMKS
2/Lt L.V. Shepherd.	Sub. Sect. Off. "B" Coy	
" T.M. Gill.	" " " B "	
" W. Megginson.	" " " C "	
" C.M. Hutchenson.	" " " C "	
" T.M. Elliot.	" " " C "	
" S.A. Welton.	" " " D "	
" T.A. Smith.	" " " D "	
" A. Cowie.	" " " D "	
" A.N. Crews.	" " " D "	
Lieut H.C. Christopherson.	Transp. Off. A Coy	
" J.H. Piperno.	" " B "	
" J.A. Shelmerdine.	" " C "	
" H.V. Everett.	" " D "	

6.9.18.

APPENDIX II.

Sheet 1.

Officers of Nº 260. M.G. Company.

- Major. H. H. Dawes.
- Capt. F. C. Runson-Baytin
- Lieut. H. C. Christopherson.
- " R. S. Withers.
- " R. B. May.
- " R. Affleck.
- 2/Lt E. C. Bradfield.
- " T. A. Smith.
- " S. A. Welton.
- " W. C. H S'wen.
- " T. A. Letheren.

17.10.15.

APPENDIX III.
Sheet. I

Officers of A Coy. 200. M.G. Battalion.

Major. W. A. Gray-Wilson.
Capt. B. F. Whiteley.
Lt. Taylor.
" E. A. Stout.
" S. C. Townend.
" R. Awde.
" Makovich.
" Broomhead.
2/Lt. Hotchkin.
" Man.
" Bruck.

COPY.   OPERATION ORDERS.   APP. IV.

No.1.

1. The Battalion will march off to entrain at Point 1.
   No. 1 Party to march off at 6-30 a.m. parade 6-0 a.m.
   No. 2 Party to march off at 10-30 a.m. parade 10 a.m.
   Composition of each party as detailed as under.

2. The camp will be ready to be handed over, an officer to be detailed by   at 10-15 a.m., all men will be clear of tents and fallen in on the parade ground by that time, except one man standing at the door of each tent, will close it up as soon as it has been inspected and fall in on parade. Special attention to be paid to out-buildings and Officers tents. Walls of tents to be pegged down.

3. Transport for No. 1 Party to be hooked in and moved on to main camp road (past camp office) facing E. at 6-15 a.m. The same detail for No 2 party at time 10-15.
   Transport Officer to be detailed later, will see that Transport lines are swept and left clean for inspection by 10-15 a.m.

4. Guides will be arranged.

5. <u>Breakfasts.</u> No. 1 Party 5 a.m. after breakfast the men will line up and draw dinner and tea rations under Coy. arrangements. Water bottles will be taken on this parade. <u>No. 2 Party</u> 7 a.m. 9 a.m. men will draw dinner and tea rations under Coy. arrangements. Water-bottles to be taken on this parade.

6. The Parties will be composed as follows:-
   <u>No.1 Party</u>   Personnel A&C Coys as per entraining orders issued at Grantham 26-9-18 except Qr.Mr. and Regt'l T.O. i.e.
   A Company 11 officers and M.O. 204 other ranks
   C   "   10 officers C.O. Asst. Adjt. 204 other ranks
   Hd.Qrs. details as detailed in above order.

   <u>Transport.</u>
       <u>1st Party</u>   <u>Vehicles</u>   A&C Coys. All Coy vehicles plus
           Bn. H.Q. G.S. Wagon i.e. 56-2wh vehicles 5-4-wh vehicles.
      <u>Horses.</u>   All Coy horses plus
          6 H.Q. horses.
              Order of march   A, C.

   <u>2nd Party.</u> Personnel as per Grantham order to include Qr.Mr. & T.O.
   O.R. same as before and H.Q. details.
   <u>Transport.</u>
   All Coy. horses and remainder of H.Q. horses.
   <u>Vehicles.</u>
   All Coy. vehicles and remainder of H.Q.

              Order of march   B, D.

   This party will also convey 33 Bicycles, rearrangement of H.Q. details will be made. A & C Coy will hand over bicycles immediately on receipt of this order to Bn Hd.Qrs.

7. <u>Blankets.</u>   Will be handed to Qr.Mr. by the first party before breakfast by Company arrangements. Time for 2nd party to be

                                                                 P.T.O.

SECRET.   Copy No. 3.

No. 200 M.G. Battalion.

OPERATION ORDERS No. 2.

1. The Battalion will relieve the 61st Machine Gun Battalion as follows:

2. Night of 2nd/3rd inst. "C" Coy. will relieve the right reserve Coy. of 61st M.G. Bn.

   Morning of the 3rd inst. "A" Coy. will relieve the left reserve Coy. of 61st M.G. Bn.

   Night of the 3rd/4th inst. "B" Coy. will relieve the left forward Coy. of 61st M.G. Bn.

   Night of the 4th/5th inst. "D" Coy. will relieve the right forward Coy. of the 61st M.G. Bn.

3. On completion reliefs will be reported to Battalion Headquarters by Runner. Immediately on completing the relief Officers Commanding Coys. will send two intelligent runners in who thoroughly understood the route to their Coy. Headquarters to Battalion Headquarters. These will bring the unexpired portion of the day's rations and will be retained at Battalion Headquarters until Battalion Runners have learned the routes to the different Coy. Headquarters, when Coy. runners will be returned to their Coys.

4. On taking up a position Officers Commanding Coys. will report personally to the Brigade Headquarters in whose area they are. The Brigades to which they are respectfully attached will be published later.

5. Intelligence Reports will be forwarded to rrach this Office (Battalion Headquarters) by 8 a.m. and 8 p.m. daily, this will not be done when actual fighting is in progress, when reports will be sent in as frequently as possible.

                              (Signed) G.I. WIEHE, Captain,
                              Adjutant No. 200 M.G. Battalion.

Issued at 1935
2-10-1918.
Copies to:-
1. Battalion H.Q.
2. R.S.M.
3. War Diary.
4.   Do.
5. O.C. "A" Coy.
6. O.C. "B" Coy.
7. O.C. "C" Coy.
8. O.C. "D" Coy.
9. Quartermaster.
10. Battalion T.O.

app. VII

SECRET.

Copy No. 7

No. 200 M.G. BATTALION.

OPERATION ORDER NO. 5

1. The following Reliefs will be carried out on the night of 13/14th October 1918:-
    "B" Company will relieve "A" Company
    "D" Company will relieve "C" Company

   Reliefs will be carried out under Company arrangements.

2. In each case the Company being relieved will take over the billet etc of the relieving Company.

3. See Operation Order No. 2, para 3, 4, & 5.

4. On completion, reliefs will be reported to Battalion Headquarters immediately by
    i. 'B' Company on relief of 'A'
    ii 'D' Company on relief of 'C'
   Code Word GOLD FLAKE (= Relief complete)

5. Trench Stores will be handed over and a copy of such forwarded to Battalion Headquarters.

6. ACKNOWLEDGE.

Issued at 1800
12-10-18

Captain,
Adjutant, No. 200 M.G. Battalion.

Distribution Normal.

add:- No. 15 No. 39 (Army) Battalion M.G.C.
       No. 16 No. 47 Battalion M.G.C.

S E C R E T.   Copy No. **6**

No. 200 M.G. BATTALION.

OPERATION ORDER No. 3.   **App. 6.**

1. The following reliefs will be carried out tomorrow, October 7th 1918. "C" Company will relieve "D" Company, "A" Company will relieve "B" Compa[ny] These reliefs will be carried out under Company arrangements.

2. In each case the Company being relieved will take over the billets etc. the relieving Company.

3. On completion reliefs will be reported to Battalion Headquarters by runner immediately.

4. See Operation Order No. 2, para 3 4 & 5.

                                            Captain,
                               Adjutant, No. 200 M.G. Battalion

Issued at
6-10-1918
Copies to:-

   No.1. 59 Div.
   No.2. 176 Brigade
   No.3. 177   "
   No.4. 178   "
   No.5. Batt. Headquarters,
   No.6. War Diary
   No.8. O.C. "A" Coy.
   No.9. O.C. "B" "
   No.10.O.C. "C" "
   No.11 O.C. "D" "
   No.12 Quartermaster
   No.13 Battalion T.O.
   No.14 R.S.M.

www.ingramcontent.com/pod-product-compliance
Lightning Source LLC
Chambersburg PA
CBHW081507160426

43193CB00014B/2613